Quilts for the Modern Home

simplify

WITH CAMILLE ROSKELLEY

Use Pre-Cut Jelly Rolls,
Charm Packs, Fat Quarters & More

stashBOOKS

an imprint of C&T Publishing

Text copyright © 2010 by Camille Olaveson Roskelley

Lifestyle photography copyright © 2010 by Camille Olaveson Roskelley

Illustrations copyright © 2010 by C&T Publishing, Inc.

Publisher: Amy Marson

Creative Director: Gailen Runge

Acquisitions Editor: Susanne Woods

Editor: Cynthia Bix

Technical Editors: Sandy Peterson and Gailen Runge

Copyeditor/Proofreader: Wordfirm Inc.

Cover/Book Designer: Kristy K. Zacharias

Production Coordinator: Kirstie L. Pettersen

Production Editor: Julia Cianci

Illustrator: Aliza Shalit

Cover photograph by Jarom William Roskelley

Published by Stash Books an imprint of by C&T Publishing, Inc., P.O. Box 1456, Lafayette, CA 94549

Library of Congress Cataloging-in-Publication Data

Roskelley, Camille.

Simplify with Camille Roskelley : quilts for the modern home - use pre-cut jelly rolls, charm packs, fat quarters & more / by Camille Roskelley.

p. cm.

ISBN 978-1-57120-938-2 (soft cover)

1. Patchwork. 2. Quilting. 3. Appliqué. I. Title.

TT835.R6745 2010

745.58'2--dc22

2010001671

Printed in China

10 9 8 7 6 5 4 3 2 1

contents

The grand and the simple. They are equally wonderful.

— Marjorie Pay Hinckley

Dedication

For my darling little boys (love you!) and my sweet husband who encouraged me to just go for it. I could never have gotten where I am today without his constant encouragement, support, and late night Dr. Pepper pick-ups.

I would also like to dedicate this to every other mom out there who wants to make something that just stays done.

Acknowledgments

A huge thank you to:

Moda Fabrics for their support, their amazing eye for design, their team of *immensely* talented designers, and the yards and yards of gorgeous fabric goodness. To Lissa, Cheryl, Mark, and everyone who makes Moda Fabrics what it is, I thank you from the bottom of my heart. Keep it up!

Bernina for making a sewing machine that could put up with me, and wonderful souls at Quiltique for making it happen and taking such good care of me.

The amazing team at C&T—Susanne, Cynthia, and each and every person who made this book what it is.

Nana for allowing my boys to make a ruckus at her home once in a while so this book could become a reality; and my mom, who taught me everything I know and who instilled in me a love and appreciation of everything handmade, for her mom who instilled it in her, and so on and so on.

foreword

Simplify. It sounds easy enough.
We all want to simplify. But where to start?

This book is all about simplicity. Simple design,
simple projects, simple fabric selection—all
coming together in a way to make the simple
life more beautiful.

My mom, Bonnie Olaveson, and me

Simplicity is the ultimate sophistication.
— Leonardo da Vinci

My family

meet the author

Quilting and design have been a part of my life for as long as I can remember. I grew up in a home that was brimming with quilts and creativity, and my mother will attest to the fact that I was constantly working on all sorts of projects (many of them secret, much to her chagrin), some turning out better than others.

When I began my company, Thimble Blossoms, my main purpose was to have an outlet—a place where I could fulfill my desire to create something original, something that would help inspire others to recognize their creative potential as well.

Since starting my business in the summer of 2007, I have designed more than 40 original quilt patterns. Every time I begin the design process, my desire is always to create something different, something special that will give other quilters—young and old, new and experienced—something to be passionate about.

My mother, Bonnie Olaveson, and I were asked to design fabric for Moda in 2008. We have designed three lines of fabric so far—Cotton Blossoms, Simple Abundance, and Bliss. Working with Moda has been an amazing experience, and we couldn't be happier about being a part of the Moda family.

I began a design and lifestyle blog in 2007 after writing a family blog for about a year, and I enjoy the creative outlet it provides. I blog about quilting, raising a family, and life in general. I also enjoy learning about photography, and I take any chance I can get to learn more. To even things out, I should probably mention that I am physically incapable of cooking a decent meal. It's true.

Being a stay-at-home mom while running a business has been quite the adventure so far, and I look forward to the (fingers crossed) many more years ahead.

www.thimbleblossoms.com
WEBSITE

www.camilleroskelley.com
BLOG

Simplify with Camille Roskelley

chapter one
quiltmaking basics

This section will guide you through the basics of quiltmaking, with a few tricks and tips along the way. It would probably be a good idea to read through this entire chapter. That way, if you have a question later, you can refer back to the section you need. Of course, if you know everything you need to know about quilting already (and I'm sure you do), just jump right into your first project! I'll be right here waiting if you have any questions.

Let's get started . . .

easy fabric selection

When I first began quilting, fabric selection seemed a little overwhelming. To walk into a store and just know what would look great together? Forget about it. Somewhere along the line I was introduced to a Charm Pack, and it was love at first sight. Each and every square in the little pack complemented the others beautifully. Genius. I still enjoy selecting fabric based on pattern, scale, and color on occasion, but I mainly stick with using one fabric collection for my design style.

Somewhere along the line I was introduced to a Charm Pack, and it was love at first sight.

Some of you may be seasoned quilters who are experts at selecting fabric, but even you have to admit, it is tough to beat the convenience of cut goods.

What are *cut goods*? The term generally refers to a specific fabric collection that is cut to specific sizes. For example, Cotton Blossoms, the first line of fabric my mother, Bonnie Olaveson, and I designed for Moda, had 40 coordinating prints. A Cotton Blossoms Charm Pack included 40 squares, each 5″ × 5″, neatly cut and ready to be sewn. (To see these fabrics in a quilt, take a look at *Coming Home* on page 51.)

cut goods rundown

CHARM PACKS

These groups of 5″ × 5″ squares of coordinating fabric come from the same collection of fabric (otherwise known as a *fabric line*). Charm Packs include one of each of the prints, usually between 25 to 40 squares. The back label typically indicates how many Charm Squares are included.

LAYER CAKES

Want to throw together a quick and easy quilt? Layer Cakes are the answer. Love 'em! These collections of 10″ × 10″ squares are from one fabric line. They used to include 40 squares, but the new ones now have 42. By the way, the photograph shows a Charm Pack on top of a Layer Cake (for size reference and because I may have forgotten to take a picture of the Layer Cake by itself).

keeping it simple

A few other fabric details: Every project in this book was made from premium-quality 100% cotton. Although many of the fabric lines are sold out now, you can find similar fabric at your local quilt store.

For the creamy neutral solids in this book, I used a Moda Bella Solid fabric called Snow.

I used Bella Solid Snow in *Square One* (full quilt on page 31).

JELLY ROLLS

Jelly Rolls are my *favorite*. They look so darn cute all rolled up. And even if I just stack them on my shelf, they are gorgeous to look at. A Jelly Roll consists of 40 strips of 2½″ × width of fabric cuts from one line of fabric.

HONEY BUNS

Like a Jelly Roll, only sweeter. And thinner. Honey Buns use the same concept as a Jelly Roll, but the 40 strips are 1½″ wide instead of 2½″. Darling, darling.

TURNOVERS

Turnovers are collections of 6″ half-square triangles of fabric. Two of each print are included, making 80 triangles per pack. So many possibilities!

keeping it simple

FYI: There is no need to prewash your cut goods. Just start sewing!

Simple as that.

FAT QUARTER BUNDLES

Okay, maybe these are my favorite. Fat quarter bundles are a stack of heaven. A bundle is a stack of fat quarters from a line of fabric, and it includes as many fat quarters as there are prints in the collection.

What is a fat quarter? Well, if you cut ¼ yard of 44″-wide fabric, it would measure 9″ × 44″. So, you'd have a long skinny quarter yard. Instead, a fat quarter is 18″ × 22″, or half the length and twice the width, which is still a quarter yard. And darn cute all stacked up.

Fat quarter bundles are a stack of heaven.

tools and cutting

ROTARY CUTTERS, MATS & RULERS

Rotary cutters might be the greatest quilting invention of all time—after the sewing machine, of course. What is a rotary cutter? It is a fantastic little tool with a handle and a circular cutting blade that rotates to cut the fabric quickly and accurately. Once you get the hang of it, you can cut through several layers of fabric at once.

caution!

Rotary cutter blades are razor sharp, so it is wise to get in the habit of retracting the blade instantly after each cut. That way you reduce the risk of finding out how sharp it really is!

When you use your rotary cutter, you'll need to use a cutting mat too. Cutting mats are made of a thick, self-healing material and are very resilient. You will also need a straight acrylic ruler that is roughly the same length as your mat. My very favorite combo is my Olfa 18″ × 24″ mat and my 2″ × 18″ ruler.

SQUARING UP FABRIC

The instructions in this book primarily use rotary cutting techniques, which means that before you begin cutting yardage or fat quarters, you will need to square up your fabric to ensure accuracy. To square up yardage, fold the fabric in half lengthwise, lining up the selvages. Place the fabric on your cutting mat with the selvages parallel to a horizontal gridline on the mat. The left edge of the fabric is where you will begin cutting, with the bulk of the fabric to the right.

Using a long, straight acrylic ruler, align the ruler vertically with a gridline on the cutting mat. Holding the ruler in place with your left hand, press firmly on the rotary cutter with your right hand and cut the uneven fabric raw edges along the ruler's right edge. Discard this cut section. Don't pick up the fabric once it has been squared up; just continue to cut the strips as directed in the project instructions.

Use a similar technique to square up fat quarters, lining up one long edge with a horizontal gridline.

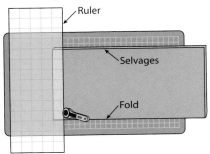

Squaring up fabric

keeping it simple

Just in case you are wondering, 1 yard of fabric is 36″ × WOF (width of fabric, from selvage to selvage). Most fabric is considered to be 44″ to 45″ wide. However, because it isn't usually quite that, I base the yardage amounts for my projects on an assumed width of 42″, to be safe. If your fabric is 45″ wide, there is no need to trim it to 42″.

Cutting Strips and Squares

When you are using yardage rather than cut goods (to make your quilt borders, for example), you'll need to cut strips, and sometimes squares, from these larger pieces of fabric.

Cutting Strips

To cut multiple strips, start at the squared edge (see Squaring Up Fabric on page 14), measure the desired width with your ruler, and cut along your ruler's right edge. After every few cuts, open the cut strips to make sure they are straight. There may be a bump in the middle along the fabric fold; if this is the case, stop cutting and square up the fabric again. This will help you get straight strips every time.

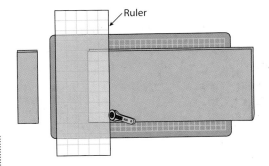

Cutting Squares

When you are cutting multiple squares, first cut a strip the appropriate width. Place the strip parallel to the horizontal markings on your cutting mat. Align your ruler with a vertical gridline on the mat near the left edge of the strip. Then trim off the selvage and square up this end. Using your ruler, measure to the correct dimension of the desired square; then cut the strip vertically along the right edge of the ruler. Repeat until you have the number of squares you need. You can cut rectangles in the same way.

THREAD

Selecting thread can be a little tricky. There are so many different kinds, so many different options. For quilting, I use 100% cotton thread because I use 100% cotton fabric. I especially enjoy Mettler 100% cotton thread and have had great luck with it.

SEWING MACHINE

When choosing a sewing machine for quilting, look for a machine with a nice straight stitch and possibly a blanket stitch for appliqué. I use a Bernina, and it puts up with me pretty well. Bernina has a wide range of sewing machines, from beginner to professional. I would definitely recommend any of them.

If your machine is struggling, you can usually solve the problem simply by rethreading the machine and changing the needle. Sewing machines also run better when serviced regularly and kept clean.

piecing basics

Ask any quilter and they will tell you that the key to exact piecing is accurate cutting, pinning, pressing, and a perfect ¼″ seam. And remember, practice makes perfect! We've already covered accurate cutting (page 14); now on to pinning, pressing, and perfect seams.

"Pin well"

Throughout this book, you will see the terms "pin well" and "pin and sew." My pinning technique is pretty simple. As a rule of thumb, I pin each and every seam intersection; when sewing smaller pieces together, I pin once at the beginning, once at the end, and once in the middle. If the pins are more than 3″ apart, add additional pins. For more on pinning borders, see Tackling Borders (page 22).

The ¹/₄″ Seam Allowance

Every time you sew two pieces of fabric together, you lose ½″. For example, two 3″ × 3″ squares sewn together would measure 5½″ across when finished. This is because in quilting you use a ¼″ seam allowance.

The easiest way to get a perfect ¼″ seam is to use your sewing machine's patchwork foot. When using this foot with your needle in the center position, the fabric only needs to be lined up with the edge of the foot.

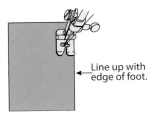

Line up with edge of foot.

To test your ¼″ seam, sew two test pieces of fabric together, taking care to line up the straight edges of the fabric pieces with the edge of your presser foot. (If you don't have a ¼″ presser foot, your sewing machine should have markings on the plate below the presser foot for you to follow.) Press the seams to one side (page 18); then with a seam gauge or ruler, measure the seam allowance. Make any necessary adjustments and restitch until the seam allowance measures ¼″ wide. (If needed, stitch again with either a bigger or smaller seam allowance to achieve the perfect size.)

The best way to get perfect ¼″ seams is to practice. Sew together test strips of fabric until you are confident in sewing straight, accurate ¼″ seams.

PRESSING

Once you have your perfect ¼" seam, you need to press it. Before you open up the stitched pieces, press the seam from the outside to set the stitches. Then open the pieces and press the seam (usually) toward the darker fabric. For most of my piecing, I use a steam iron or the steam setting on my regular iron. Press as you go along, seam by seam. Don't wait to press two crossing seams at once; it will never lie flat and straight.

Generally speaking, when two seams are joined—for example, when you are sewing together two rows of squares to make a block—they should be pressed in opposite directions to create a *locking seam* (also called a *nesting seam*). Doing this will greatly improve your piecing accuracy.

In general, plan ahead to alternate directions of pressed seams that meet in adjacent blocks or rows so that they nest when they meet and are sewn together.

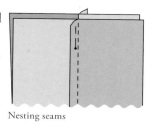

Nesting seams

CHAIN PIECING

Chain piecing simply means feeding the units to be sewn through your sewing machine one after another, without stopping to cut the threads between each unit. Once you have a chain of sewn pieces, snip the threads between the units and press. This is a huge timesaver that can greatly speed up the piecing process.

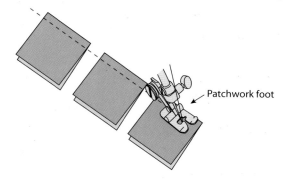

Patchwork foot

APPLIQUÉ AND FUSIBLE WEB

Of the many different appliqué methods available, the one I use throughout this book is the fusible web method. I find it to be the quickest, easiest method for appliqué, and certainly the most beginner-friendly. Fusible web is an iron-on adhesive that holds the fabric appliqué to the quilt so that the appliqué can be stitched on. I use a paper-backed adhesive fusible web called HeatnBond Lite (make sure it is Lite!) for all of my appliqué.

note

All the appliqué patterns in this book have been *reversed* so you can trace them directly onto the paper side of the fusible web. (The monogram on page 81 is the exception. Please follow the special monogram instructions on page 84 to apply the letters.)

My fusible web appliqué technique is a quick five-step method.

1. Trace the pattern from the project instructions directly onto the paper side of the fusible web. Cut out the shape, leaving about ¼″ of fusible web around the *outside* of the traced line of each shape.

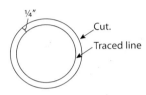

2. Cut out the center of the shape to reduce bulk, leaving another ¼″ of fusible web on the *inside* of the traced line. Think of it as a shape outline, rather than a solid piece.

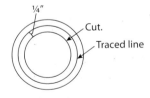

3. With the paper side up of the fusible web, and using your iron, follow the manufacturer's instructions to apply the fusible web to the back of the designated fabric for the appliqué. Cut out the shape on the traced line. Remove the paper.

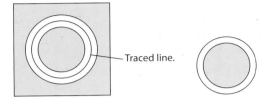

4. Using your iron for the length of time instructed on the fusible web package, apply the fused appliqué piece to the quilt top.

5. Blanket stitch around each shape, either by machine or by hand.

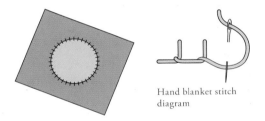

Hand blanket stitch diagram

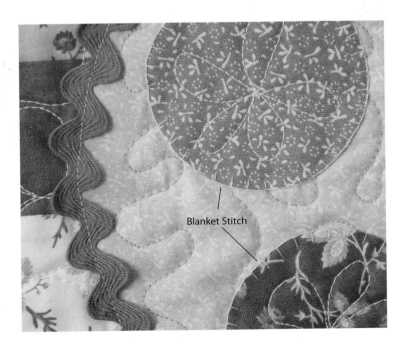

Simplify with Camille Roskelley

chapter two
finish it!

Once you get the center of your quilt pieced, it may be tempting to fold it up nicely and put it away for another day. I know I've been tempted to do just that. Although putting on borders can be a bit of a pain, it's not nearly as bad as it seems (no pun intended). Follow these steps to finish your quilts and say goodbye to the closet.

tackling borders

Borders are definitely not my favorite part of the quilting process, but they are certainly a necessity. I've found that if I can get my borders on the right way each time, it makes all the difference in the quilt's overall look.

CUTTING STRIPS

To start, cut the number of strips indicated in the project instructions at the width that is called for. If the sides of the quilt are longer than about 44", you'll need to sew two border strips together end to end for each side. I sew the seam straight across the border pieces, perpendicular to the long edges.

MEASURING AND PINNING

To attach the borders correctly, you will need accurate measurements of your particular quilt top. For this reason, I don't give the exact border measurements for the quilt projects in this book.

The first step in preparing your borders is to measure your quilt from top to bottom along each side and once down the center. The three measurements should be the same. If they aren't quite the same, take the average of the three lengths and place a pin to mark that length measurement on each of the two side border strips. (This pin marks one end of the border strip; the other end is the cut edge at the other end of the strip.)

Fold the border strips in half crosswise by aligning the marked pin at one end with the other cut end of the strip to find the center. Similarly, fold the quilt top in half to find the center of the side edges. With the centers and both ends aligned (remember one end of the border strip was previously marked with a pin), pin the borders to the sides of the quilt top. Add more pins to secure the side border strips to the quilt, distributing the fabric evenly across the quilt top. (You will trim the borders after they are stitched.)

STITCHING

Sew the borders in place, trim off any excess fabric from the ends, and press the seams toward the outside edges of the borders. While the quilt is on the cutting mat, make sure the corners are square.

Repeat the process for the remaining top and bottom borders. To reduce waste and simplify, you may need to add the trimmed portions of the side border strips to the remaining strips cut for the top and bottom borders to make the strips long enough. (Remember to include the side borders in the quilt top's three width measurements.)

See, it's not so bad. And the best part? Perfect borders, every time.

batting

I typically recommend 100% cotton batting, such as Warm & Natural (or Warm & White for a white quilt top). I occasionally use an 80%-20% cotton-polyester blend for a slightly thicker quilt. But as a general rule for quilting, I stick with a thin, low- to medium-loft cotton batting.

backing

The backing is a piece of cake to put together. Just follow the project instructions to cut the correct lengths of fabric, remove the selvages, and then pin and sew a straight line, right sides together, where you trimmed away the selvages. Press the whole thing. For quilts smaller than 44″ wide, use a single width of fabric that is cut to the correct length.

If you are machine or hand quilting, your backing and batting need to be at least *2″ bigger on all sides* than your quilt top. If you are having it quilted by a longarm quilter (page 26), it should be 4″ bigger on all sides, but ask your quilter before preparing your quilt back.

making a quilt sandwich

To make a quilt sandwich, layer the back, batting, and quilt top and prepare your creation for quilting.

1. Place the freshly ironed backing wrong side up on a flat surface, such as a clean floor or large table. Use masking tape to secure it to the surface every 8″ or so. Make sure the backing is taut but not stretched.

2. Center and smooth the quilt batting in place on top of the backing.

3. Center the quilt top, right side up, on the quilt batting and smooth out any wrinkles, making sure the top edge of the quilt top is parallel with the backing's top edge.

4. Starting in the center of the quilt, use curved safety pins (they make life so much easier!) to baste together the 3 layers for machine quilting. Pin every 4″ or so, covering the quilt top.

For hand quilting, use a long needle and thread, rather than safety pins, to baste the layers together. Baste horizontally and vertically on a grid with stitching lines about 4″ apart and ¼″ from each edge.

quilt as desired

Oooh, I *love* to machine quilt! Machine quilting offers so many options and endless possibilities. I'll cover just a few favorites here.

You'll need a special foot for machine quilting. Shown here are a walking foot (for straight line quilting) and two darning feet (for freehand quilting).

Open- and closed-toe darning feet

Walking foot

STIPPLING

Stippling is random, allover freehand stitching in whatever pattern you choose. Use a darning foot and be sure to lower the feed dogs on your sewing machine. Start in the top right corner and work your way down to the opposite corner, filling in as you go. A few favorites:

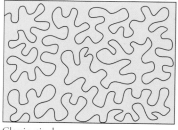

Classic stipple

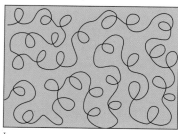

Loops

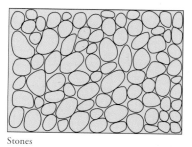

Stones

MODERN LINE QUILTING

A new favorite of mine is quilting in rows, either evenly spaced or randomly. This adds a modern flair to a design, whether modern or traditional. A walking foot is a necessity for this kind of quilting, and painter's tape can be a huge help. Just place the tape in straight lines on the quilt top; then follow the tape edge with the edge of your walking foot.

Evenly spaced lines

Random straight lines

Outline quilting

A simple way to quilt is to stitch ¼" from each seam or appliqué shape. Outline quilting highlights the quilt's design elements and should be done with a walking foot, if possible.

HAND QUILTING

I am far from an expert at hand quilting, but I certainly appreciate the skill behind it, as well as the beauty it gives a quilt. Hand quilting resembles a running stitch that penetrates all three layers. Use a single strand of 100% cotton quilting thread to sew ¼" away from each seam or to create intricate designs. It's all up to you! Remove the thread basting when you've finished hand quilting your project. (For more about hand quilting from an expert, refer to *Hand Quilting with Alex Anderson*, available from C&T Publishing.)

LONGARM QUILTING

A few of the quilts in this book were quilted by a professional using a longarm quilting machine. Longarm quilting is done on a machine where the quilt is stationary and the machine moves. It is especially helpful with larger quilts. If you are having your quilt professionally quilted, there is no need to baste. Check with your quilter for specific instructions.

After you have completed the quilting (by whatever method), trim the backing and batting even with the quilt top edges, making sure your corners are square.

binding

My favorite binding is called a double-fold binding with mitered corners. It is quick and easy, and it gives a nice, crisp edge.

To bind your quilt, follow these steps:

1. Using your cutting mat, ruler, and rotary cutter, cut the number of strips needed for the project 2½″ × WOF.

2. With right sides together, sew the binding strips end to end, straight across, to make one long strip. Press the seams open.

3. Press the strip in half lengthwise, wrong sides together.

4. Start stitching the binding to the quilt at the center of one side of the quilt, leaving a 6″ tail of binding. Stitch the binding to the front of the quilt, aligning raw edges, through all layers, using a ¼″ seam.

5. When you approach a corner, stop ¼″ before the corner. Backstitch and then remove the quilt from beneath the presser foot. To miter the corner, fold the binding up to create a 45° angle, making sure the next quilt edge and binding form a straight line.

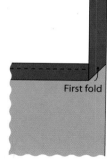

First fold

6. Hold the first fold in place as you fold and bring the binding back down in line with the next quilt edge. Start stitching at the top of the fold and continue stitching on this side of the quilt. Repeat at all corners.

Second fold

Sweet Pea (full quilt on page 45)

7. When you come back to where you started, stop stitching 6″ before the end. Fold the ending tail of the binding back on itself where it meets the beginning binding tail. Finger-press. From this fold, measure and mark the cut width of your binding strip. Cut the ending binding tail to this measurement.

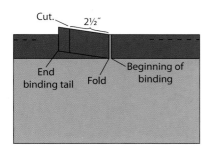

8. Open both tails. Place one tail on top of the other at right angles, right sides together. Pin. Mark a diagonal line and stitch on the line. Trim the seam allowance to ¼″. Press open.

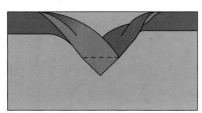

Connect ends.

9. Refold the binding and continue stitching it to the quilt. After the binding is machine stitched to the front of the quilt, bring the folded edge around to the back of the quilt, miter the corners, and hand stitch in place.

BIAS BINDING

Whenever you are binding a project that doesn't have a straight edge, you need to use a bias binding instead of a double-fold binding. When you prepare a bias binding, you will cut the strips at a 45° angle from the selvage, instead of across the straight grain of the fabric. After cutting the strips, you can continue following the basic binding instructions.

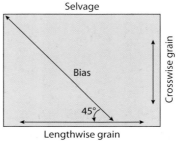

Cutting on the bias

camille's tips for simplifying your life

Reduce clutter. Take 20 minutes a day to clean out a drawer, a purse, or a closet. Weeding out clutter will help reduce stress while keeping things organized.

Take an afternoon off of your normal routine and make time for a favorite book, a favorite outing—or a favorite stack of fabric.

Limit your to-do list to three larger tasks per day. If you accomplish more than this, you will be overachieving, rather than falling short!

Organize your life with one calendar. One quick glance in the morning can help you plan out your day in just a few moments.

Don't over-schedule! Easier said than done, right? Evaluate your weekly activities and decide which are essential. If possible, try to schedule your day with plenty of time between events. That way you can go through the day at a more leisurely pace, instead of rushing from one appointment to the next.

Create dedicated family time. We have planned family time every Monday night. We enjoy a fun activity as a family, figure out what everyone has going for the week, and just enjoy one another's company. Some family activities: a quick game of tag or kickball, go for a walk, play board games, or barbecue.

Surround yourself with your favorite things.

This quilt has a fun, scrappy look, achieved with Charm squares and Honey Bun strips, plus a raw-edge binding made of strips of the leftover Honey Bun strips to top it all off.

Square one. It's a perfect place to start. Maybe a little overwhelming, maybe a little scary, but definitely exciting.

square one

Pieced and quilted by Camille Roskelley

Finished quilt size: 56½″ × 65″   Finished block size: 6½″ × 6 ½″

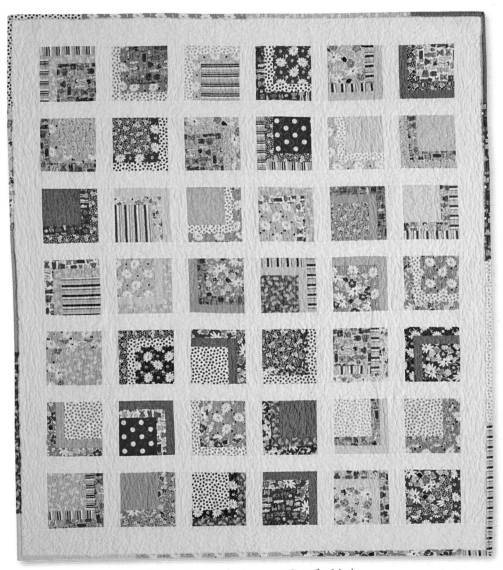

Fabric: Snippets by American Jane for Moda

One of my very favorite things is helping others learn a new skill—namely, quilting! In fact, I have a little blue sewing machine at my house for just that purpose. Little Blue is all about square one. When a friend wants to give quilting a try, she comes over, gets a crash course in piecing, starts her first quilt top, and takes home Little Blue. This little machine has visited so many homes, I've lost track, but she never stays for too long. See, it's never very long before the new quilter catches the quilting bug and gets a machine of her (or his) own. And then it's back to square one for Little Blue.

keeping it simple

If you don't have enough squares in your favorite Charm Pack, simply buy an extra fat quarter or two (or more) and cut extra 5″ × 5″ squares until you have enough for your project. Scatter the squares throughout the quilt to create a unifying element, not to mention a one-of-a-kind quilt.

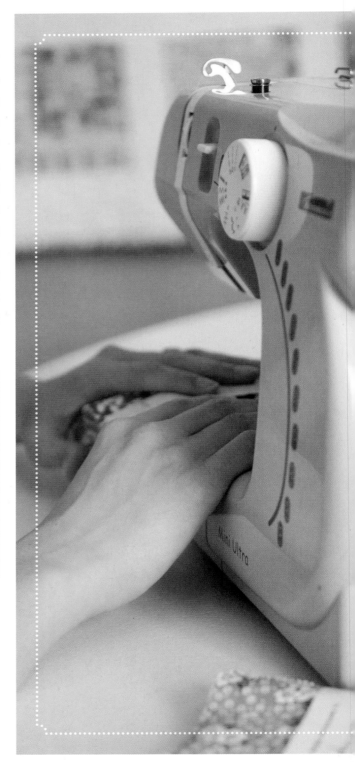

Materials

Yardage requirements are based on 42″-wide fabric.

1 Charm Pack or 42 Charm Squares 5″ × 5″ for the blocks

1 Honey Bun or 40 strips of fabric 1½″ × WOF for the blocks and binding

2 yards neutral fabric at least 42″ wide for the sashing and borders

3⅝ yards fabric for the backing

Warm & Natural batting: 61″ × 69″

keeping it simple

Cut your time in half by lining up the Honey Bun strip pairs on your cutting mat and cutting several at once. You'll have your quilt cut out in no time!

Cutting

1. Pair up the Honey Bun strips into 20 sets of 2. Label one fabric in each set A and the other fabric B. Cut each Honey Bun strip into 4 pieces: one 5″, two 6″, and one 7″ rectangle per strip. (Keep these pieces together as sets.)

| 1½″ | 5″ | 6″ | 6″ | 7″ | |

2. From the neutral fabric, cut 15 sashing strips 2½″ × WOF and 6 strips 4″ × WOF for the borders. Subcut 6 of the 2½″ strips into 7″ × 2½″ rectangles. Cut 6 rectangles per strip until you have a total of 35. Set aside the remaining strips.

Block Assembly

Note: All sewing is done right sides together with ¼" seam allowances, unless otherwise noted.

The ability to simplify means to eliminate the unnecessary so that the necessary may speak.

— Hans Hofmann

1. Select a Charm Square. Choose a set of Honey Bun pieces. From the A fabric, choose a 5" rectangle and a 6" rectangle. From the B fabric, choose a 6" rectangle and a 7" rectangle. Set aside the remaining pieces from this set for the next block.

2. To assemble the block, refer to the block assembly diagram below. Pin and sew the 5" (A) rectangle to the left side of the Charm Square. Pin and sew the 6" (A) rectangle along the top.

3. Pin and sew the 6" (B) rectangle to the left side of the block. Finally, pin and sew the 7" (B) rectangle to the top to complete the block. Each block measures 7" × 7" square, unfinished.

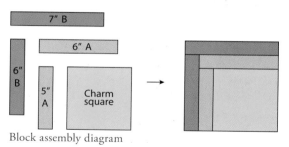

Block assembly diagram

4. Repeat Steps 1–3 with a second Charm Square, using the leftover strips from fabrics A and B from Step 1. However, reverse the order so that the B fabrics (5" and 6" rectangles) are applied first, and then the A fabrics (6" and 7" rectangles). It'll work; trust me.

5. Repeat Steps 1–4 to make a total of 40 blocks. From the Honey Bun scraps, cut enough A and B fabric rectangles for 2 more blocks. As before, assemble the blocks so you have a total of 42.

Quilt Top Assembly

To assemble your quilt top, refer to the quilt assembly diagram below. Each row uses 6 blocks and 5 rectangles 2½″ × 7″ of the neutral sashing that you cut earlier.

1. Lay out the blocks in 7 rows of 6 blocks each, rotating the blocks randomly until they look the way you like (see the quilt on page 31). There is no right or wrong way.

2. To assemble the first row, alternate the blocks and the 2½″ × 7″ sashing rectangles. Pin and sew a rectangle to the right side of the first block, then pin and join the second block, and so on, ending with the sixth block. Repeat to assemble 7 rows.

3. To connect the rows, sew together the remaining 2½″ sashing strips end to end. As with Tackling Borders (page 22), measure the length of rows 1 and 2, take the average, measure a strip of the sashing the same length as this average, and mark the length on the long sashing strip with a pin. Aligning centers and ends, pin and sew the sashing strip along the bottom of row 1. Similarly, pin and sew row 2 along the bottom of the sashing strip. After pressing, trim the sashing even with the side of the quilt top. Use the trimmed sashing strip between rows 2 and 3 of the quilt top.

4. Continue sewing the rows and sashing strips together until you have 7 rows of blocks and 6 rows of neutral sashing.

5. For the borders, sew together 2 of the 4″ neutral fabric strips end to end for each side of the quilt top. As described in Tackling Borders (page 22), measure the sides of the quilt top. Measure 2 border strips the same length and mark with a pin. Aligning centers, pin and stitch them in place. After pressing, trim the side borders even with the top and bottom of the quilt top. Add each of these 2 trimmed pieces to each of the remaining 2 border strips. As before, add these border strips to the top and bottom of the quilt top.

Quilt assembly diagram

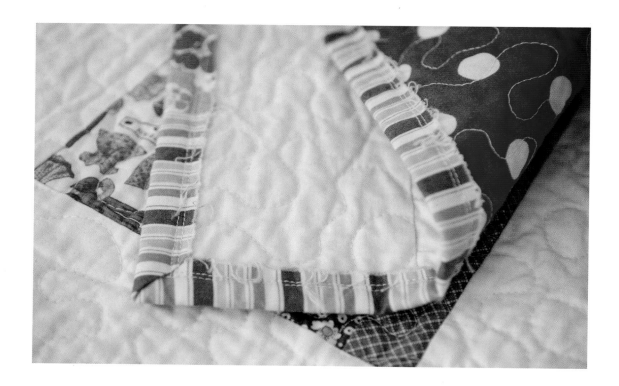

Finishing

1. Cut the backing fabric into 2 equal lengths (each at least 61″). Trim off the selvages and sew together the 2 pieces to make a large piece at least 61″ × 69″.

2. Make a quilt sandwich (page 23). Then machine or hand quilt as desired. Trim any excess and square up the corners.

3. For the raw edge binding, sew your remaining Honey Bun strips end to end until you have one long strip at least 265″. Fold the binding in half lengthwise (right side out). Press the entire length. To sew the binding to the quilt, start about 6″ from a corner, and wrap the binding around the quilt edge, with one side of the fold on each side of the quilt. Sew ¼″ from the binding's edge through all layers, leaving a raw edge on the binding. Stop stitching about ½″ from the next corner and remove the quilt from the sewing machine. Adjust miters on both the front and back of the quilt and resume stitching. Continue around the quilt. When you return to the beginning, simply overlap the binding ends by about an inch and trim off the excess.

Our home is full of miniature racecars, Legos, and baseballs—everything boy. My little boys had so much fun "helping" me put this quilt together, and I have the feeling it won't be the last *Little Man* quilt at our house.

I have two amazing little men in my life at the moment, and I couldn't be happier about it.

little man

Pieced and quilted by Camille Roskelley

Finished quilt size: 40½″ × 51½″   Finished block size: 10″ × 10″

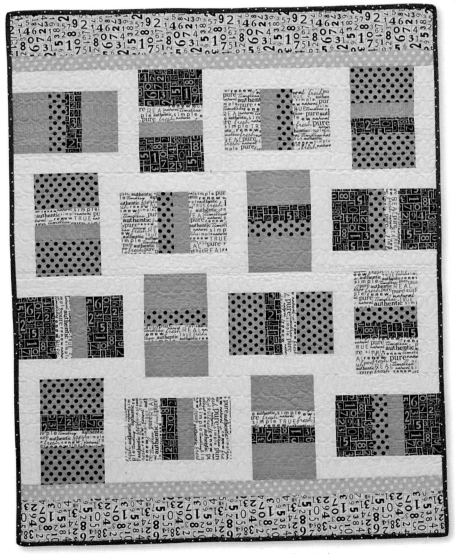

Fabric: au*then*tic by Sweetwater for Moda

This quilt design really shows off a fabric line—in this case, the perfect fabrics for a "simple" quilt (literally; read the words on the fabric!). Each block is a mix-and-match combination of three different fabrics from your fat quarter stash. A double border on top and bottom is the perfect finishing touch.

keeping it simple

Keep in mind that almost any quilt can be made bigger or smaller just by adding or taking away a row or two of blocks. This block would make a great picnic quilt, lap quilt, or even—gasp!—little *girl* quilt made out of only the sweetest pinks and reds.

Materials

Yardages are based on 42″-wide fabric.

4 fat quarters

¾ yard neutral fabric at least 42″ wide for the blocks

¼ yard fabric for the inner border

⅜ yard fabric for the outer border

1¾ yards fabric for the backing

½ yard fabric for the binding

Warm & Natural batting: 45″ × 56″

Cutting

1. From the neutral fabric, cut 8 strips 2½" × WOF. Subcut each strip into 4 rectangles 10½" × 2½" until you have 32. Label these rectangles B.

2. From each fat quarter, lay out and cut rectangles and strips as shown below: 4 rectangles (C) 6½" × 8" and 8 strips (A) 2" × 6½".

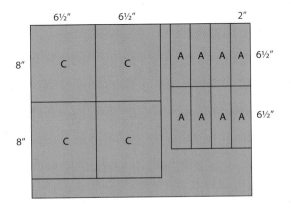

3. Cut each 6½" × 8" (C) piece in half as shown to create 2 rectangles (D) 6½" × 4".

Block Assembly

Note: All sewing is done right sides together with ¼" seam allowances, unless otherwise noted.

Each block is made of two rectangles from one fabric and two strips, each from a different fabric, bordered on top and bottom with a neutral fabric.

1. Refer to the block assembly diagram below as you assemble the block: Take 2 D rectangles from the same fabric and sew each to an A strip from 2 different fabrics along their 6½" sides. Join the 2 units by sewing together the long edges of the 2 A strips.

2. Pin and sew a 10½" × 2½" rectangle (B) to each long side of the unit from Step 1 to create a 10½" × 10½" (unfinished) block.

3. Make 16 blocks.

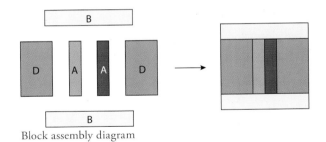

Block assembly diagram

Quilt Top Assembly

1. Sew together the blocks in 4 rows of 4 blocks, rotating every other block as shown in the quilt assembly diagram (below). Sew the 4 rows together to make the quilt top center.

2. From the inner border fabric, cut 2 strips 2″ × WOF. Measure the top and bottom of the quilt top, and then measure 2 border strips the same length (see Tackling Borders, page 22). Mark with a pin. Pin and sew one border strip along the top and one along the bottom of the quilt top.

3. From the outer border fabric, cut 2 strips 4½″ × WOF. Again, measure the top and bottom of the quilt top, and then measure 2 border strips the same length. Mark with a pin. Pin and sew one border strip along the top and one along the bottom of the quilt top.

Finishing

1. Make a quilt sandwich (page 23). The backing may not be 4″ wider than the quilt top, but why waste fabric? Machine or hand quilt as desired.

2. For the binding, cut 5 strips 2½″ × WOF and continue as instructed in Binding (page 26).

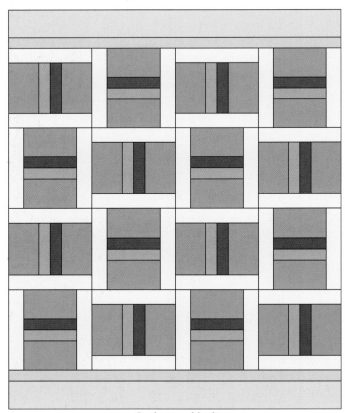

Quilt assembly diagram

There's nothing sweeter than a little baby girl quilt. Well, except possibly a sweet baby girl. I absolutely love to sew girly little quilts. There is something about pink, red, aqua, ribbon and scallops that tug at my heart strings.

This is the perfect size for a crib quilt. This crib quilt features a charming scalloped edge (see the patterns on page 104) and a bias binding.

The finishing touch? The sweet ribbon that ties it all up like a gift.

sweet pea

Pieced and quilted by Camille Roskelley

Finished quilt size: 42″ × 42″   Finished block size: 3½″ × 3½″

Fabric: from my scrap bag

keeping it simple

When your scrap bag is overflowing, one way to tame it is to cut it into 5″ × 5″ squares and then sew up your favorite Charm Pack pattern like I did to make this quilt. You are guaranteed to have a one-of-a-kind project.

Materials

Yardage for this quilt is 44″ wide.

2 Charm Packs or 64 squares 5″ × 5″ for the blocks

1 yard white fabric for the inner and outer borders

⅓ yard aqua fabric for the middle border

1½ yards fabric for the backing (It'll be tight!)

½ yard fabric for the bias binding (or 5½ yards of purchased bias binding)

1½ yards 1″-wide ribbon

Warm & Natural batting: 46″ × 46″

Cutting

1. Divide your Charm Squares into 32 pairs. Each pair is one set. In each set, place one square on top of the other, *right sides up.*

2. Cut each set of squares into 2 strips 2¼″ × 5″, 2 strips 1½″ × 5″, and 2 strips 1¼″ × 5″.

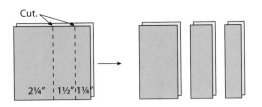

3. Lay out the strips and swap the center 1½″ strips in each combination.

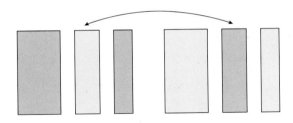

Block Assembly

Note: All sewing is right sides together with a ¼″ seam allowance, unless otherwise noted.

These super-simple blocks are each composed of three strips.

1. Sew each block together as follows: sew the 2¼″ strip to the 1½″ strip and then to the 1¼″ strip. Press. You now have a block that measures 4″ × 5″. Trim it to measure 4″ × 4″.

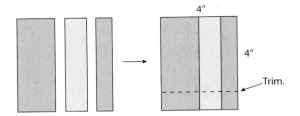

2. Repeat to make a total of 64 blocks.

Quilt Top Assembly

1. Sew the blocks in 8 rows of 8, alternating the orientation of the blocks so they are random. Pin and sew the rows together to make the quilt top.

2. To make the ribbon embellishment, cut a 9″-long piece of ribbon and a 2½″-long piece of ribbon. For the bow, mark the center of the 9″ piece and fold each end under toward the center, overlapping at the center by ¼″. Pin.

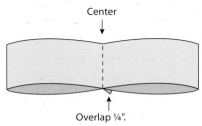

Fold ribbon toward center and overlap ¼″.

3. Pin and sew the remaining ribbon to the quilt top, overlapping rows 7 and 8. Topstitch by machine along each edge of the ribbon all the way across the quilt top. Wrap the 2½″ piece of ribbon around the center of the bow and pin where desired. Topstitch around the "knot."

4. For the narrow inner borders: From the white border fabric, cut 3 strips 1½″ × WOF. Measure the sides of the quilt top (see Tackling Borders, page 22) and measure 2 border strips the same length. Mark the border strips with a pin. Pin and stitch these border strips in place. Trim. Sew the 2 trimmed border pieces to the remaining border strip and cut the strip in half crosswise. As before, measure the correct lengths and sew the borders to the top and bottom of the quilt top. Make sure the corners are square.

5. For the middle border: From the aqua border fabric, cut 4 strips 2¼″ × WOF. As before, measure the sides of the quilt top and measure 2 border strips the same length. Mark the border strips with a pin. Pin and stitch these border strips in place. Trim. Repeat to add the top and bottom borders. Make sure the corners are square.

6. From the remaining white fabric, cut 4 strips 4½″ × WOF. As before, measure the sides of the quilt top and measure 2 border strips the same length. Mark the border strips with a pin. Pin and stitch them in place. Trim. Repeat to add the top and bottom borders. Make sure the corners are square.

7. Enlarge and trace the scallop pieces from the patterns (page 104) onto a piece of paper. (Enlarge and trace 8 Sweet Pea Border Scallop patterns and 4 Corner Border Scallop patterns.) Cut out the pieces. Place a corner scallop piece on one corner of the quilt top, lining up the border lines with your middle border. Line up the other scallop pieces until you reach the next corner.

You may have to adjust slightly, as your quilt top may be a slightly different size. Continue placing the paper pieces all around the quilt top, adjusting as needed. Use a water-soluble fabric pen to trace the outer scallop shapes onto the outer white borders. Do *not* cut along the traced line until after the quilt is quilted and you are ready to apply the binding.

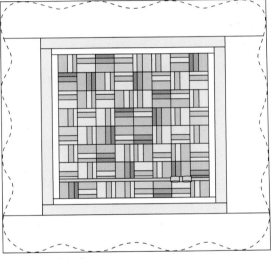

Quilt assembly diagram

Finishing

1. Make a quilt sandwich (page 23) and machine or hand quilt as desired. Trim along the traced scallop line. Note that in this case, my backing is a little smaller than usual, but why waste fabric? If your back is just a bit smaller than your quilt top, scoot your scallop a bit toward the center. The best part? No waste!

2. For the binding, refer to Bias Binding (page 27) to cut 2½″ strips on the bias at a 45° angle until you have 5½ yards of binding. Continue as instructed in Binding (page 26) to sew on the binding. For this quilt, gently ease the binding around the curves as you stitch it to the quilt front and tuck as necessary on the inner angles when you turn it to the back.

The large white borders are the perfect spot to showcase some favorite quilting: flowers, loops, swirls, or something even fancier. Go nuts!

I can never seem to have too many table toppers. They are the absolute perfect afternoon project. I love to switch mine out often, and I enjoy making them for friends and family. Because they're small, they can be finished much more quickly than a full-size quilt, and they make the perfect housewarming gift, birthday gift, or any gift for that matter.

To me, it's the little finishing touches around the house that make coming home feel like home.

coming home

Pieced and quilted by Camille Roskelley

Finished quilt size: 36½″ × 36½″   Finished block size: 4½″ × 4½″

Fabric: Cotton Blossoms by Bonnie and Camille for Moda

Materials

Yardages are based on 42″-wide fabric.

1 Charm Pack or 36 squares fabric 5″ × 5″ for the blocks

¾ yard neutral fabric for the blocks and inner border

½ yard aqua fabric for the outer border

1⅜ yards for the backing

⅜ yard for the binding

Warm & Natural batting: 41″ × 41″

Cutting

From the neutral fabric, cut 5 strips 2¼″ × WOF. Subcut each strip into 2¼″ × 2¼″ squares until you have 72 squares. On the wrong side of each square, use a pencil to draw a diagonal line from one corner to the opposite corner.

Block Assembly

Note: All sewing is done right sides together with ¼″ seam allowances unless otherwise noted.

keeping it simple

Remember to press seams in opposite directions and pin well, especially anytime you have two points that are supposed to meet up. Just remember to pull out the pins right before they go under the presser foot. Your sewing machine will thank you!

1. On each of the 36 squares for the quilt center, pin 2 squares 2¼″ × 2¼″ of the neutral fabric in opposite corners, right sides together.

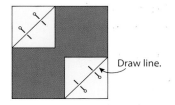

Draw line.

2. Sew along your pencil lines; then trim off the corners ¼″ from the seam. Open and press the seams in the same direction.

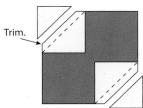

Trim.

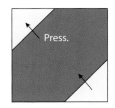

Press.

3. Repeat to make a total of 36 blocks.

Quilt Top Assembly

1. Refer to the quilt assembly diagram below as you sew the blocks in 6 rows of 6, alternating the blocks to create locking seams (page 18). Sew the rows together.

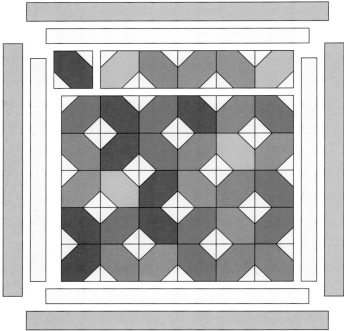

Quilt assembly diagram

Finishing

1. Make a quilt sandwich (page 23) and machine or hand quilt as desired.

2. For the binding, cut 4 strips 2½″ × WOF and continue as instructed in Binding (page 26).

2. From the remaining neutral fabric, cut 4 strips 2½″ × WOF for the inner border. Measure the sides of the quilt top (see Tackling Borders, page 22). Measure 2 inner border strips the same size and mark the inner border strips with a pin. Pin and stitch them in place. Repeat for the top and bottom inner borders.

3. From the aqua outer border fabric, cut 4 strips 3″ × WOF. As before, measure the sides of the quilt top. Measure 2 outer border strips the same size and mark the outer border strips with a pin. Pin and stitch them in place. Repeat for the top and bottom outer borders.

Take one look around my home and you'll notice a trend. I love dots. Big dots, little dots, but most especially polka dots. I have polka dot quilts, table toppers, shirts, dresses, shoes, towels, casserole dishes, and even furniture (!). This dot quilt was made in a pretty, traditional colorway, but it would also be great made out of some funky fabric—like your little guy's favorite space fabric or the sweetest spring line—with aqua sashing.

There's no doubt about it— Everything is better with polka dots.

spot on

Pieced by Camille Roskelley
and quilted by Tami Bradley

Finished quilt size: approximately 59½″ × 75″   Finished block size: 9½″ × 9½″

Fabric: Glacé by 3 Sisters for Moda

The large dots on this quilt are appliquéd onto square blocks—simple! The blocks are set on-point and connected with diagonal sashing. You'll find the circle pattern on page 104. Enlarge the pattern 200% for this quilt.

Materials

Yardages are based on 42"-wide fabric.

1 Layer Cake or 41 squares various fabrics 10" × 10"

1 yard red fabric for the sashing

⅝ yard fabric for the inner border

1 yard fabric for the outer border

3¾ yards fabric for the backing

⅝ yard fabric for the binding

Warm & Natural batting: 64" × 79"

1¾ yards fusible web (I use HeatnBond Lite.)

Cutting

Enlarge and trace 17 circles from the pattern (page 104) onto the paper side of the fusible web. Cut out the circles, reduce bulk in the center of the circles, and apply the fusible web to the back of each of 17 Layer Cake squares, following the fusible web instructions (page 18). Cut out the circles and remove the paper from the back of the fusible web.

Block Assembly

1. Apply a finished circle in the center of 17 of the remaining Layer Cake squares.

2. Using your machine's blanket stitch or stitching by hand (see page 19), stitch around each circle.

3. Cut an additional 7 Layer Cake squares in half diagonally, from one corner to the opposite corner.

Quilt Top Assembly

Note: All sewing is done right sides together with ¼″ seam allowances, unless otherwise noted. There are 7 diagonal rows in this quilt top.

1. Cut 14 strips of sashing fabric 2″ × WOF. Subcut 6 of the strips into 10″ × 2″ strips until you have 24. Then cut 2 strips 3″ long and 2 strips 25″ long. Sew the remaining strips together end to end and cut 2 strips 50″ long and 2 strips 72″ long. Note that these lengths are generous.

2. Lay out the squares, triangles, and strips as shown in the quilt assembly diagram (page 60). Sew the diagonal rows first; the 2 triangles in the bottom left corner form the first row. Sew a 2″ × 10″ sashing strip between these 2 pieces. Continue making diagonal rows as shown in the diagram, sewing the 2″ × 10″ sashing strips between the blocks.

3. When you have completed sewing all 7 diagonal rows, sew the rows together. Again, start with the bottom left corner and sew the 8 sashing strips to the diagonal rows, using the longer sashing strips as the rows become longer. Remember to sew the 2 shortest sashing strips (3″ long) to the outside corners of the first and last diagonal rows.

4. Trim the sides to make them straight and trim the 3″ sashing strips in the bottom left corner and the top right corner to square up the corners.

5. From the inner border fabric, cut 6 strips 3″ × WOF. For each side of the quilt, sew 2 inner border strips together end to end lengthwise. Refer to Tackling Borders (page 22) to measure the sides of the quilt top. Measure 2 inner border strips the same size and mark them with a pin. Pin and stitch them in place. Trim the inner borders and add each of the trimmed pieces to each of the remaining inner border strips. Repeat the process to add the top and bottom inner borders with the remaining strips.

6. From the outer border fabric, cut 7 strips 4½″ × WOF. For each side of the quilt top, sew 2 border strips together end to end lengthwise. As before, measure the sides of the quilt top. Measure 2 outer border strips the same size and mark them with a pin. Pin and stitch them in place. Trim the outer borders. Join the remaining 3 outer border strips together end to end to make one long strip. Cut the strip in half crosswise. Repeat the process to add the top and bottom borders to the quilt top.

Finishing

1. Cut the backing fabric into 2 equal lengths (each at least 64″). Trim off the selvages and sew together the 2 pieces to make one large piece at least 64″ × 79″.

2. Make a quilt sandwich (page 23) and machine or hand quilt as desired.

3. For the binding, cut 7 strips 2½″ × WOF and continue as instructed in Binding (page 26).

Row 7

Row 1

Quilt assembly diagram

I heart throw pillows; just ask my husband. There isn't a horizontal surface in our home that isn't covered with them. Okay, maybe there aren't quite that many, but I definitely have more throw pillows than I can count. The thing I love about them is that it is so easy to change the feel of a room just by adding a few fresh pillows.

So make up a few, or a few hundred. I won't tell.

toss-up pillows

Pieced and quilted by Camille Roskelley

You have a choice of pillows to make in four different designs and three different sizes—two are 16″ × 16″ finished, one is 14″ × 14″ finished, and one is 13½″ × 13½″ finished. Each pillow coordinates with one of the quilts in this book.

Fabric: Rouenneries by French General for Moda

spot on pillow

Finished pillow size: 13½″ × 13½″

Spot On features nine Charm Squares, each with a large dot fused and appliquéd to the center. The pattern (page 105) is sized at 100%; do *not* enlarge it for the circles on this pillow. The pillow is quilted using an allover "stones" design (page 24).

Materials

18 Charm Squares 5″ × 5″

1 fat quarter for the pillow back

1 piece of muslin 16″ × 16″ for the quilt sandwich

Warm & Natural batting: 16″ × 16″

1 pillow form: 14″ × 14″

⅓ yard fusible web (I use HeatnBond Lite.)

note

All sewing is done right sides together with ¼″ seam allowances, unless otherwise noted.

Pillow top assembly

1. Trace 9 circles from page 105 on to the paper side of the fusible web (for more fusible web tips, see page 18). Fuse a fusible web circle on the back center of each of 9 Charm Squares, following the fusible web manufacturer's instructions. Cut out the circles and remove the paper. Fuse a finished circle in the center of each of the remaining 9 Charm Squares.

2. Using your machine's blanket stitch or stitching by hand (page 19), stitch around each circle.

3. Sew together the blocks in 3 rows of 3. Press seams in adjacent rows in alternate directions (page 18). Pin and sew the rows together to create a nine-patch.

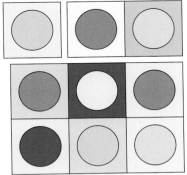

Pillow top assembly diagram

Finishing

To finish your pillow, cut 2 pillow back pieces 14″ × 9″ from the fat quarter. Then follow the general pillow finishing instructions (page 71).

keeping it simple

What do you do with all those bits and pieces of fabric left over from your projects? Put them to use! These pillows, which feature blocks from other quilts in the book, are a great way to use up your leftover Charm Squares, Jelly Rolls, Layer Cakes, and so forth.

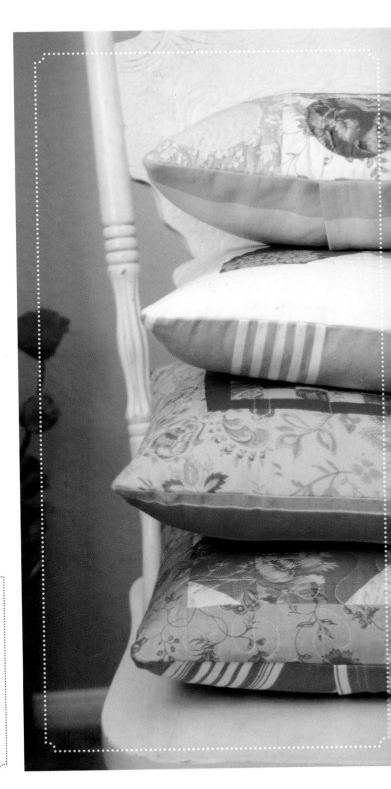

coming home pillow

Finished pillow size: 14″ × 14″

Here's a pillow-sized version of my *Coming Home* quilt (page 50). The straight-line quilting gives it a clean, modern feel.

Materials

4 Charm Squares 5″ × 5″

⅓ yard neutral fabric for the blocks and border

1 piece muslin 16″ × 16″ for the quilt sandwich

1 fat quarter for the pillow back

Warm & Natural batting: 16″ × 16″

1 pillow form: 14″ × 14″

Pillow top assembly

1. From the neutral fabric, cut 2 strips 3″ × WOF. Subcut the strips to yield 2 strips 9½″ × 3″ and 2 strips 14½″ × 3″. From the leftover fabric, cut 8 squares 2¼″ × 2¼″. On the back of each square, draw a diagonal pencil line from one corner to the opposite corner.

2. On each of the four 5″ Charm Squares, pin 2 neutral 2¼″ squares in opposite corners, right sides together.

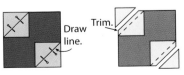

Corner unit

3. Sew along the pencil line, then trim off the corners ¼″ from the seamline on the outer side. Open and press the seams in the same direction.

4. Refer to the pillow top assembly diagram below as you pin and sew the blocks in 2 rows of 2, alternating the directions of the seam allowances to create locking seams (page 18). Sew the rows together.

5. Pin and sew a 9½″ × 3″ strip to each side of the pillow top center. Pin and sew a 3″ × 14½″ strip to the remaining 2 sides.

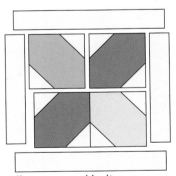

Pillow top assembly diagram

Finishing

To finish your pillow, cut 2 pillow back pieces 14½″ × 9″ from the fat quarter. Then follow the general pillow finishing instructions (page 71).

dream big pillow

Finished pillow size: 16″ × 16″

This fun, super-simple pillow has a center of 64 little squares surrounded by an inner border and a wide outer border. Modern line quilting (page 25) gives it a fresh look.

Materials

64 squares coordinating fabrics 1½″ × 1½″ (or leftover Honey Bun strips)

⅛ yard fabric for the inner border (or 1 Honey Bun strip)

⅓ yard fabric for the outer border

1 piece muslin 18″ × 18″ for the quilt sandwich

1 fat quarter for the pillow back

Warm & Natural batting: 18″ × 18″

1 pillow form: 16″ × 16″

Pillow top assembly

1. Lay out the 1½″ × 1½″ squares in 8 rows of 8, rearranging them until you are satisfied with the color balance. Sew them together in rows. Press, alternating the direction of the seams with adjacent rows. Pin and sew the rows together to create the pillow top center. Press well! The center measures 8½″ × 8½″, including seam allowances.

2. From the inner border fabric or Honey Bun strip, cut 2 strips 8½″ × 1¼″ and 2 strips 10″ × 1¼″. Pin and sew an 8½″ strip to each side of the pillow top center and a 10″ strip to each of the remaining 2 sides.

3. From the outer border fabric, cut 2 strips 3¾″ × WOF. Subcut the strips to yield 2 strips 10″ × 3¾″ and 2 strips 16½″ × 3¾″. Pin and sew a 10″ strip to each side of the pillow center and a 16½″ strip to each of the remaining 2 sides.

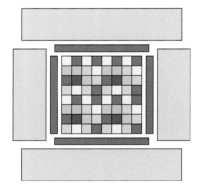

Pillow top assembly diagram

Finishing

To finish your pillow, cut 2 backing pieces 16½″ × 11″ from the fat quarter. Then follow the general pillow finishing instructions (page 71).

happy-go-lucky pillow

Finished pillow size: 16″ × 16″

This is a simple red-and-neutrals version of the *Happy-Go-Lucky* quilt (page 80). A quilting pattern of classic stippling (page 24) finishes off the four-block pillow top.

Materials

4 Jelly Roll strips 2½″ × 42″

4 squares 2½″ × 2½″ of coordinating fabrics

8 squares 2″ × 2″ of neutral fabric

1 fat quarter for the border

1 fat quarter for the pillow back

1 piece of muslin 18″ × 18″ for the quilt sandwich

Warm & Natural batting: 18″ × 18″

1 pillow form: 16″ × 16″

Pillow top assembly

1. Cut each Jelly Roll strip to yield 2 rectangles 6½″ × 2½″ and 2 squares 2½″ × 2½″. These are referred to as Fabric 1. The other four 2½″ squares of coordinating fabric are called Fabric 2.

2. Each block has 3 rows. To assemble a block, start with the center row. Pin and sew a 2½″ Fabric 2 square between two 2½″ squares of Fabric 1. Sew a 6½″ strip of Fabric 1 to each side of the center row.

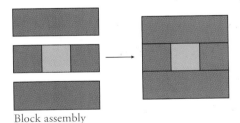

Block assembly

3. Repeat Step 2 to assemble 4 basic blocks.

4. On each of the 8 neutral 2″ squares, draw a diagonal pencil line from one corner to the opposite corner. Pin a 2″ neutral square in each corner of 2 of the basic blocks. Sew along the pencil lines and trim off the corners ¼″ from the seams to make 2 pieced blocks.

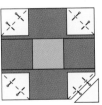

Add corner units.

5. Alternating between the basic blocks and the pieced blocks with the corner units, sew 2 rows of 2 blocks, alternating the direction of the seam allowances to create locking seams (page 18). Sew the rows together.

6. Cut the fat quarter for the border to yield 2 strips 12½″ × 2½″ and 2 strips 16½″ × 2½″. Pin and sew the 12½″ strips to the sides of the pillow center. Pin and sew the 16½″ strips to the remaining 2 sides.

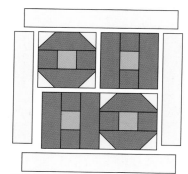

Pillow top assembly diagram

Finishing

To finish your pillow, cut 2 pillow back pieces 16½″ × 11″ from the fat quarter. Then follow the general pillow finishing instructions (page 71).

Finishing the Pillows

All of the pillows are finished the same way. The only difference is in the finished sizes. *Make sure you cut the pillow back piece to the correct dimension for the pillow you are finishing.*

1. Make a quilt sandwich (page 23) with the pillow top, batting, and the piece of muslin. Quilt by machine or by hand, as desired.

2. Fold under a long edge of each pillow back piece (to the wrong side) ⅛″ and press. Fold again to the wrong side to make a hem: Sew a 1″ hem on one piece and a ¾″ hem on the other piece. Press. With the quilted pillow top right side up, place the pillow back pieces on top, right sides down, aligning raw edges with the quilted pillow top. The 2 back pieces overlap. Pin all around the raw edges.

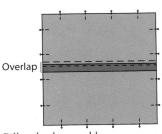

Overlap

Pillow back assembly

note

The bigger the overlap of the back pieces, the better. Once the pillow form is inside, you don't want to see it.

3. Sew a ¼″ seam all the way around the raw edges of the pillow twice, taking care to reinforce the 4 pillow corners and the areas where the 2 flaps overlap. Turn the pillow cover right side out. Insert the pillow form.

tip

You can easily add or remove stuffing from the pillow forms to give the pillows the shape you like. Some forms have a zipper. For others, you may need to open a seam and then stitch it closed after you remove the innards. I actually removed a little bit of stuffing from the pillow form in the 13½″ finished pillow so it wasn't quite so full.

Repeat until you have so many pillows you can't sit on your couch!

I don't know what it is, there is just something so sweet about a scallop! Add a scrumptious Moda Jelly Roll and a few simple flowers to the mix, and you have yourself a sugar rush. The best possible kind of sugar rush of course.

Add a bit (or a lot) of chocolate, and you are all set!

sugar rush

*Pieced by Camille Roskelley
and quilted by Tami Bradley*

Finished quilt size: 56½″ × 75½″

Fabric: Patisserie by Fig Tree Quilts for Moda

Scalloped and outer borders

1. From the neutral fabric, cut 3 strips 7½″ × WOF. Sew them together end to end. Cut this long strip into 2 pieces 7½″ × quilt center width.

2. This part is a little tricky! Enlarge and trace the scallop from the pattern on page 105 onto the paper side of the fusible web 10 times. Referring to Appliqué and Fusible Web (page 18), cut the pieces apart. Trim the scalloped edges. Cut 2 scallops in half crosswise down the center. These will be used for the ends of the scalloped border at each side of the quilt (see the quilt photograph, page 73).

3. For each border, line up the fusible web scallop pieces, paper side up, along the back of the neutral strips to make the scalloped borders shown in the quilt assembly diagram (page 77). Make two continuous scallop series that start and end with the half scallops. Adjust to fit.

4. Following the manufacturer's instructions, press the fusible web pieces to the back of the neutral fabric. Trim along the curved lines of the scallop pieces to remove excess fabric. Remove the paper.

5. From the red outer border fabric, cut 3 strips 15″ × WOF. Sew them together end to end lengthwise. Refer to Tackling Borders (page 22) to cut 2 pieces the same length as your quilt center width.

6. Fuse a scalloped border piece to the *right* side of each of the red outer border strips, lining up the straight edge of the scallop piece with a long edge of the outer border.

7. Using your machine's blanket stitch or stitching by hand (page 18), stitch the first scalloped border to the red outer border along the scalloped edge only, along the entire length. Repeat for the second scalloped border.

8. Pin and sew the border units to the top and bottom of the quilt as shown in the quilt assembly diagram.

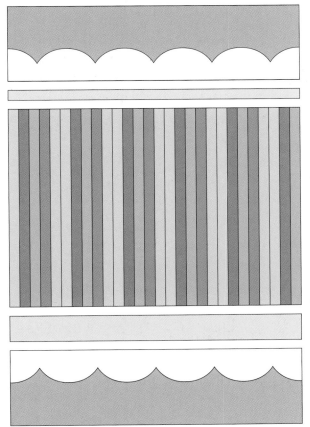

Quilt assembly diagram

Life is really simple, but we insist on making it complicated.

— Confucius

APPLIQUÉING THE FLOWERS

1. Enlarge and trace 1 of each of the 6 flower patterns (pages 105–107) onto the paper side of the fusible web. Trim out the fusible web from the centers of the shapes (see Appliqué and Fusible Web, page 18). Fuse these flower pieces to the wrong side of the flower appliqué fabrics—the 2 largest shapes onto the 2 fat quarters and the remaining shapes onto the fat eighths.

2. Cut out the flower shapes and the flower centers. Remove the paper from the back of the fusible web and place the flowers on the quilt top where desired, using the quilt photograph (page 73) as a guide. Fuse the flowers to the quilt top. Stitch around each shape, using your machine's blanket stitch or stitching by hand (pages 18–19).

Finishing

1. Cut the backing fabric into 2 equal lengths (at least 61″). Trim off the selvages and sew together the 2 pieces to make one large piece at least 61″ × 80″.

2. Make a quilt sandwich (page 23) and machine or hand quilt as desired.

3. For the binding, cut the remaining Jelly Roll strips in half crosswise and sew 14 strips together end to end. Continue as instructed in Binding (page 26).

I'm not sure what it is about this quilt, but I was so happy when I was putting it together. The blocks came together quickly and perfectly, it was sunny outside, I had some of my favorite music playing and a nice cold Dr. Pepper to keep me company. At that moment, I didn't have a care in the world. Life was good.

hap•py-go-luck•y -adjective, trusting cheerfully to luck; unworried or unconcerned.

happy-go-lucky

Pieced by Camille Roskelley
and quilted by Tami Bradley

Finished quilt size: 63½″ × 75½″   Finished block size: 6″ × 6″

Fabric: 1974 by Urban Chiks for Moda

This happy arrangement of blocks is subdivided by horizontal and vertical bands of solid fabric sashing, giving it a bold, different look.

keeping it simple

The monogram block (pattern on page 108) is optional. You will have enough blocks to fill the space if you choose to leave it out. If you use the monogram, use your extra blocks to make the Happy-Go-Lucky pillow (page 69).

Materials

1 Jelly Roll or 40 strips 2½″ × WOF coordinating fabrics for the blocks (strips assumed to be at least 41″ long)

⅝ yard neutral fabric at least 40″ wide for the blocks and the optional monogram

½ yard purple fabric for the sashing

1⅓ yards fabric for the border

4 yards fabric for the backing

¾ yard fabric for binding

2 fat quarters (for optional monogram)

⅓ yard fusible web (for optional monogram)

Warm & Natural batting: 68″ × 80″

Cutting

1. Cut each Jelly Roll strip into 4 rectangles 6½″ × 2½″ and 6 squares 2½″ × 2½″.

Note: Cut carefully! There will be very little waste.

2. From the neutral fabric, cut 5 strips 2″ × WOF. Subcut each strip into 2″ × 2″ squares until you have 96. Using a pencil, lightly draw a diagonal line from one corner to the opposite corner on the back of each square.

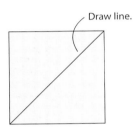

Draw line.

3. For the monogram (optional), cut 1 square 8½″ × 8½″ from the neutral fabric. Cut 2 strips 8½″ × 2½″ and 2 strips 12½″ × 2½″ from one fat quarter.

Block Assembly

Note: All sewing is done right sides together with ¼″ seam allowances, unless otherwise noted.

Each of the 80 blocks is made up of 2 Jelly Roll print fabrics. Each block is made up of 3 rows. Twenty-four of the blocks (the B blocks) have 4 corners of the neutral fabric.

MAKING THE A BLOCKS

1. Before sewing anything, make a stack of fabric for each block containing 2 different prints from the Jelly Roll fabrics:

> From Fabric 1: 2 rectangles 6½″ × 2½″ and 2 squares 2½″ × 2½″
>
> From Fabric 2: 1 square 2½″ × 2½″

2. To assemble a block from one stack, pin and sew a 2½″ Fabric 1 square to 2 opposite sides of a 2½″ Fabric 2 square to make the center strip. Sew one 6½″ Fabric 1 strip to each side.

3. Continue to assemble blocks until you have 80 A blocks.

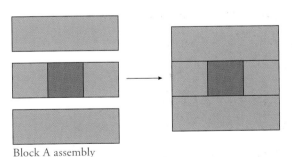

Block A assembly

1. Choose 24 of your assembled A blocks. Pin a 2″ neutral fabric square in each corner. Sew along the pencil lines and trim ¼″ from the seamline toward each corner.

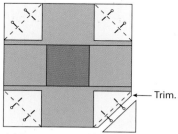

← Trim.

Add corners to B blocks.

2. Repeat until you have completed 24 blocks. You now have 56 A blocks and 24 B blocks.

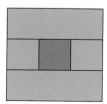

Block A

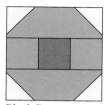

Block B

Making the monogram block (optional)

Sew an 8½″ strip of the monogram print fabric to each side of an 8½″ square of neutral fabric. Press. Sew a 12½″ strip of monogram print fabric to the top and bottom.

making a monogram

To create your monogram letter, you can either

- Use a copy machine to enlarge and print one of the letters from the alphabet on page 108 until it is 5½″ tall; or

- Open your computer's word-processing program and type your letter (upper- or lower-case). Then choose a font you like and change the font size until your letter measures approximately 5½″ tall; then print.

Trace the outline of your letter on the back of a piece of paper to create a reversed image. (Cross out the printed letter on the front so you aren't tempted to trace it.) Trace the outline of your (backward) letter onto the paper side of the fusible web and follow the appliqué instructions (see Appliqué and Fusible Web on page 18), using your remaining fat quarter to create and fuse your monogram to the neutral fabric.

Quilt Top Assembly

ASSEMBLING THE QUILT CENTER

Option 1 (with Monogram)

To make this option, you'll sew the quilt center together in 3 sections, as shown in the quilt center diagram and described below.

1. For Section 1, sew the blocks together in 5 rows of 6 blocks each, alternating between A blocks and B blocks. Sew the rows together.

2. For Section 2, sew the alternating blocks as shown. Sew blocks 1 and 2 together; then sew them to the left side of the monogram block. Sew together blocks 3–5 and 6–8 in 2 rows of 3 blocks each. Sew the rows together, and then sew them to the right side of the monogram block.

3. For Section 3, sew a row of 6 blocks, alternating between A and B blocks.

4. Sew the 3 sections together to create the quilt center.

Option 2 (without Monogram)

For the quilt center, sew together 8 rows of 6 blocks each, alternating between A blocks and B blocks.

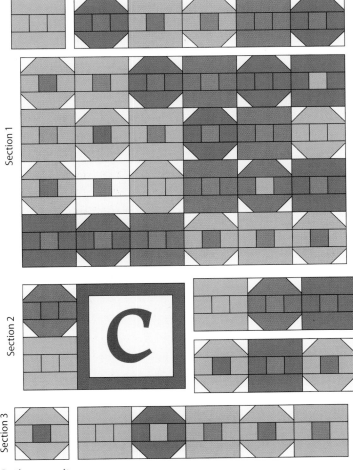

Quilt center diagram

ASSEMBLING THE QUILT TOP

Adding the Sashing

1. From the purple sashing fabric, cut 6 strips 2½" × WOF.

2. Sew together 3 sashing strips end to end. Refer to Tackling Borders (page 22) to measure the sides of the quilt center (they should measure 48½"). Measure 2 sashing strips the same length; pin and sew them to the sides.

3. Sew together 2 rows of 8 remaining A blocks. Pin and sew them to the outside edges of the side sashing strips. Trim the sashing.

4. Measure the top and bottom of the quilt center (they should measure 52½"). Sew together 3 sashing strips end to end. Measure 2 sashing strips the same length; pin and sew them to the top and bottom. Trim the sashing.

5. From the trimmed sashing strips, cut 4 strips 6½" × 2½". For the top and bottom of the quilt center, refer to the quilt assembly diagram at the right and sew 2 rows as follows: one A block, one 2½" sashing strip, 6 A blocks, one 2½" sashing strip, and one final A block. Pin and sew a row to the top of the quilt and the other row to the bottom.

Adding the Outer Borders

1. From the outer border fabric, cut 7 strips 6" × WOF.

2. Sew together 2 outer border strips end to end for each side of the quilt. As before, measure the sides of the quilt. Measure 2 border strips the same size and mark with a pin. Pin and stitch them in place. Trim.

3. Sew together the remaining outer border strips end-to-end. Add the trimmed pieces from the side borders.

4. As before, measure the width of the quilt. Measure 2 border strips the same size and mark with a pin. Pin and stitch them in place to add the top and bottom borders to the quilt top. Trim.

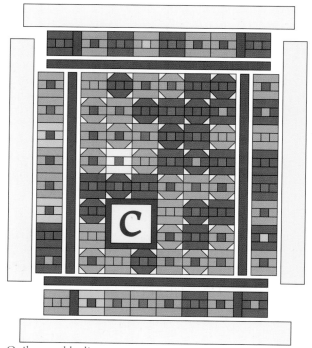

Quilt assembly diagram

Finishing

1. Cut the backing fabric into 2 equal lengths (at least 68″). Trim off the selvages and sew together the 2 pieces to make one large piece at least 68″ × 80″.

2. Make a quilt sandwich (page 23) and machine or hand quilt as desired.

3. For the binding, cut 8 strips 2½″ × WOF and continue as instructed in Binding (page 26).

I know of at least four generations of quilters who came before me, making me at least a fifth-generation quiltmaker. My 83-year-old grandmother, an excellent quilter, was taught by her mother, who was taught by her mother. My grandmother passed on her love and knowledge of quilting to my mother, who then passed it on to me.

Quilting is in my blood.

all in the family

Designed by Camille Olaveson Roskelley, pieced
by Bonnie Beesley Olaveson, quilted by Wendy
Anspatch, and bound by Phyllis Beesley Moss

Finished quilt size: 63½″ × 71½″   Finished block size: 8″ × 8″

Fabric: Simple Abundance by Bonnie & Camille for Moda

My mom, Bonnie Olaveson, started her pattern company, Cotton Way, more than twenty years ago. Watching her design process was always fascinating to me as a child and inspired me to start my company, Thimble Blossoms. We have had the privilege of working on many projects together, and we've worked as a team designing fabric for Moda, which has been an absolute dream come true for us.

This quilt is made from our second line of fabric, Simple Abundance, and was pieced by my very own mother and bound by my sweet grandmother.

I am so proud of my heritage and thankful for the amazing women before me who passed down such a strong love and appreciation of quilting to their children. I'll try my hardest to do the same.

keeping it simple

Passing a love of sewing on to your kids may be easier than you think. Don't be afraid to start them out young! My boys love it when I give them a Charm Pack to arrange on the floor. After the squares are arranged "just so," they help me with some (supervised) pinning. Then I sew the squares together. A little stippling and binding later, and they have a new quilt to wrap themselves in or to wrap around their favorite stuffed animals— not to mention a mom who couldn't be prouder.

Materials

Yardages are based on 42″-wide fabric.

1 Jelly Roll for the blocks (28 strips 45″ long or 34″ strips 38″–44″ long)

1⅝ yards neutral print background fabric for the blocks

½ yard red fabric for the inner border

1½ yards aqua fabric for the outer border

⅝ yard red fabric for the binding

4 yards fabric for the backing

Warm & Natural batting: 68″ × 76″

Cutting

1. Cut 21 strips 2½″ × WOF from the neutral background print. Cut 16 squares 2½″ × 2½″ from each strip until you have 336 squares.

2. If your Jelly Roll strips are 38″–44″ long, then from each of 34 strips, cut 10 squares 2½″ × 2½″ and 10 squares 1¼″ × 1¼″ to make a total of 340 squares of each size, including 4 extra of each size. If your strips are 45″ long, then from each of 28 strips, cut 12 squares 2½″ × 2½″ and 12 squares 1¼″ × 1¼″ to make a total of 336 squares of each size.

Block Assembly

Each block is made up of 4 four-patch units. Each unit consists of 2 small pieced squares 2½" × 2½" and 2 plain squares 2½" × 2½".

1. Draw a pencil line diagonally, corner to corner, across the wrong side of all the 1¼" × 1¼" squares.

2. To make the small pieced squares, place a 1¼" × 1¼" square on the corner of a 2½" × 2½" neutral fabric square, right sides together. Stitch on the drawn line. Trim the seam to ¼", open the corner, and press toward the darker fabric. Repeat, using all the neutral squares and all the 1¼" squares.

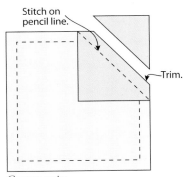

Corner units

3. To make a four-patch unit, select 2 plain squares and 2 pieced squares from matching fabric from Step 2. Sew them together as shown. The pieced blocks form a bowtie in the center.

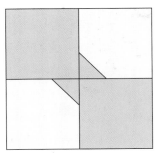

Four-patch unit

4. Make 3 more four-patch units, using coordinating fabric colors. To make a block, lay out 4 coordinating four-patch units and rotate each unit to form a "circle" of neutral fabric in the center. With right sides together, stitch together the top 2 units. Repeat with the bottom 2 units, pressing the center intersecting seams in opposite directions (page 18). Sew the 2 rows together. The block measures 8½" × 8½", including seam allowances. Repeat with different fabric squares to make 42 blocks in color-coordinated groups of 4 four-patch units.

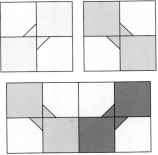

Finished block

Quilt Top Assembly

1. Lay out the blocks in 7 rows of 6 blocks each. With right sides together, stitch together 6 blocks to form a row. Repeat to make 7 rows. Press the seams in opposite directions in adjacent rows.

2. With right sides together, stitch together the 7 rows to make the center of the quilt top.

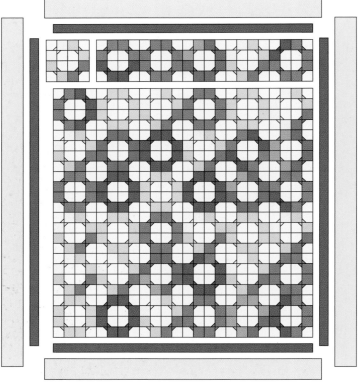

Quilt assembly diagram

3. From the red inner border fabric, cut 6 strips 2″ × WOF. Sew 2 border strips together end to end for each of the top and bottom inner borders of the quilt. Refer to Tackling Borders (page 22)

to measure the width of the quilt. Measure 2 border strips the same size and mark with a pin. Pin and stitch them in place. Trim the border strips. Sew each of the trimmed pieces to each of the remaining side inner border strips. As before, sew the side inner border strips to the quilt top.

4. From the aqua outer border fabric, cut 7 strips 6½″ × WOF. Sew 2 border strips together end to end for each of the quilt's top and bottom outer borders. As in Step 3, measure the width of the quilt. Measure 2 border strips the same size and mark with a pin. Pin and stitch them in place on the top and bottom of the quilt top. Trim. Sew the remaining strips together end to end. Add the trimmed pieces from the top and bottom borders to the remaining long strip. As before, measure and sew the side outer border strips to the quilt top. Trim.

Finishing

1. Cut the backing fabric into 2 equal lengths (at least 68″). Trim off the selvages and sew together the 2 pieces to make one large piece at least 68″ × 76″.

2. Make a quilt sandwich (page 23) and machine or hand quilt as desired.

3. For the binding, cut 7 strips 2½″ × WOF and continue as instructed in Binding (page 26).

It has been years since I first sketched this quilt. I kept putting it aside for later, because I thought it would be too complicated—too big a project. But when I sat down one day to figure it out, I realized that it wasn't complicated at all, if I just took it one row at a time. It reminded me a little bit of life and all the craziness that makes it what it is. Things are sometimes too complicated when looked at as a whole, but if you take them one step at a time, they often come together exactly as you hope—sometimes even better.

The moral of the story? Never be afraid to dream big.

dream big

Pieced and quilted by Camille Roskelley

Finished quilt size: 60½″ × 68½″

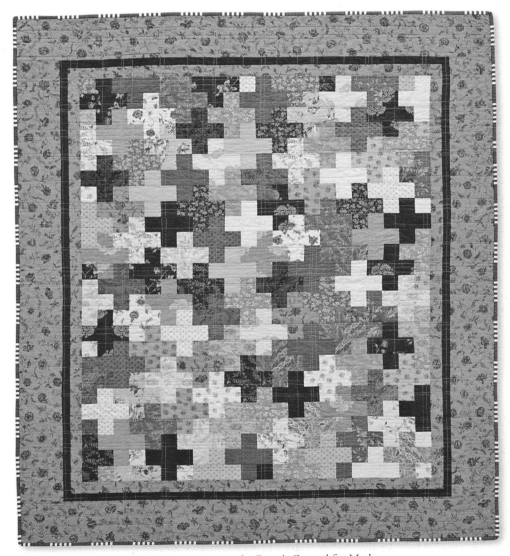

Fabric: Rouenneries by French General for Moda

keeping it
simple

Live simply,

Laugh often,

Love deeply,

Dream big.

Materials

Yardages are based on 42"-wide fabric.

1 Jelly Roll or 40 strips 2½" × WOF of coordinating fabrics

1⅝ yards fabric for the first and third gray borders

⅓ yard fabric for the second red border

⅝ yard fabric for the binding

3¾ yards fabric for the backing

Warm & Natural batting: 65" × 73"

My aim is to put down on paper what I see and what I feel in the best and simplest way.

— Ernest Hemingway

Cutting

1. Cut 28 of the Jelly Roll strips into 3 rectangles 6½" × 2½" and 7 squares 2½" × 2½".

2. Cut 10 of the Jelly Roll strips into 2 rectangles 6½" × 2½", 1 rectangle 4½" × 2½", and 6 squares 2½" × 2½".

| 6½" | 6½" | 4½" | | | | 2½" | | | | |

3. The 2½" cut squares (2" finished) are referred to as A squares; the 4½" cut rectangles (4" finished), as B rectangles; and the 6½" rectangles (6" finished), as C rectangles.

Quilt Top Assembly

Note: All sewing is done right sides together with ¼" seam allowances, unless otherwise noted.

Laying out all the pieces of the quilt center is the trickiest part of the assembly. The pieces are organized into an interlocking pattern that forms crosses based on the chosen fabric colors. Start with the full block in the top left corner (see the quilt center assembly diagram, page 101).

Each main block is made of two A squares and one C rectangle, all from the same fabric. A pair of main blocks fit together as shown.

1. Lay out all the main blocks, as indicated in the quilt center assembly diagram (outlined in aqua).

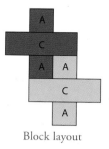

Block layout

2. Fill in the spaces around the main blocks with the remaining pieces as shown. The B rectangles go down the sides and the C rectangles go along the top and bottom. The A pieces are interspersed all around the quilt center. Maintain the color pattern. (You cut 16 extra "A" squares to help.)

3. Using a water-soluble fabric-marking pen, number each successive horizontal row on the first left-hand piece of the row from 1 to 26. Sew together the pieces in a row in order from left to right. Press, alternating the direction of the seams from row to row—to the right on row 1, to the left on row 2, and so on. This will create locking seams and will help things line up much better.

4. Sew the rows together.

5. From the gray fabric for the first and third borders, cut 6 strips 2″ × WOF for the first border. Sew 2 border strips together end to end for each side of the quilt. Refer to Tackling Borders (page 22) and measure the sides of the quilt. Measure 2 border strips the same size and mark with a pin. Pin and stitch them in

place. Trim strips. Add each of the trimmed pieces to each of the remaining 2 border strips. Repeat to add the top and bottom borders with the remaining strips.

6. From the red second border fabric, cut 6 strips 1½″ × WOF. As before, sew 2 border strips together end to end for each side of the quilt. Measure, mark, sew, and trim the borders as in Step 5. Remember to add the trimmed pieces to the remaining 2 border strips for the top and bottom borders.

7. From the remaining gray border fabric, cut 6 strips 6″ × WOF for the third border. Sew 2 border strips together end to end for each side of the quilt. Measure, mark, sew, and trim the borders as in Step 6 and add the top and bottom borders to the quilt top.

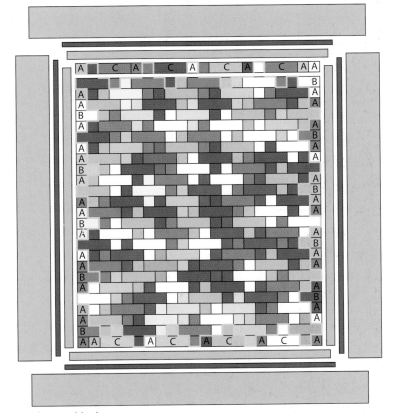

Quilt assembly diagram

Finishing

1. Cut the backing fabric into 2 equal lengths (at least 65″ long). Trim off the selvages and sew together the 2 pieces to make one large piece at least 65″ × 73″.

2. Make a quilt sandwich (page 23) and machine or hand quilt as desired.

3. For the binding, cut 7 strips 2½″ × WOF and continue as instructed in Binding (page 26).

patterns

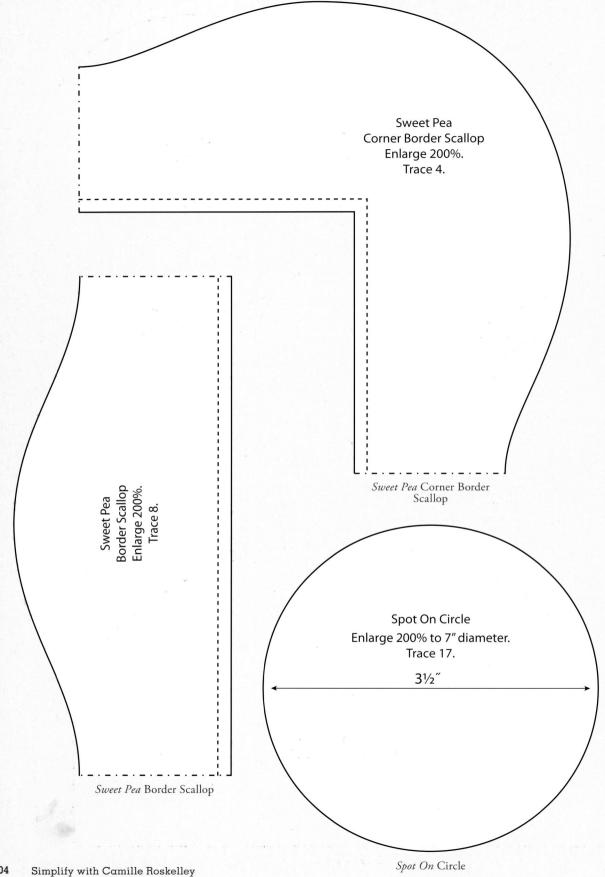

Sweet Pea
Corner Border Scallop
Enlarge 200%.
Trace 4.

Sweet Pea Corner Border
Scallop

Sweet Pea
Border Scallop
Enlarge 200%.
Trace 8.

Spot On Circle
Enlarge 200% to 7" diameter.
Trace 17.

3½"

Sweet Pea Border Scallop

Spot On Circle

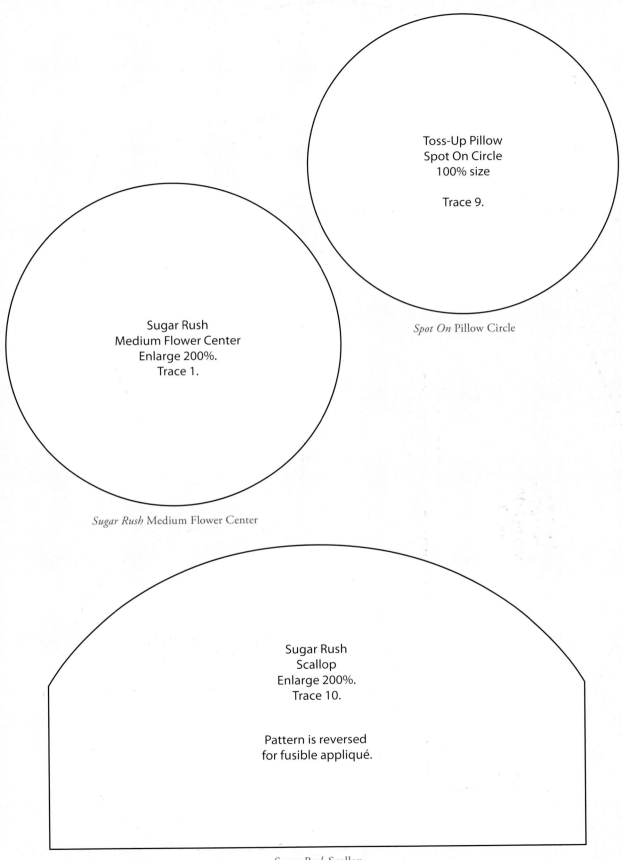

Toss-Up Pillow
Spot On Circle
100% size

Trace 9.

Spot On Pillow Circle

Sugar Rush
Medium Flower Center
Enlarge 200%.
Trace 1.

Sugar Rush Medium Flower Center

Sugar Rush
Scallop
Enlarge 200%.
Trace 10.

Pattern is reversed
for fusible appliqué.

Sugar Rush Scallop

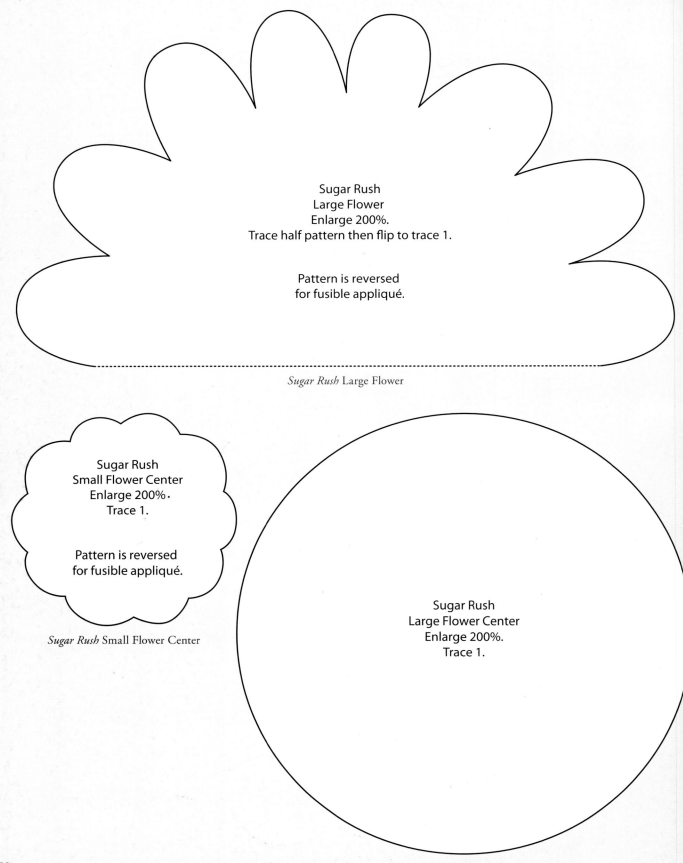

Sugar Rush
Large Flower
Enlarge 200%.
Trace half pattern then flip to trace 1.

Pattern is reversed
for fusible appliqué.

Sugar Rush Large Flower

Sugar Rush
Small Flower Center
Enlarge 200%.
Trace 1.

Pattern is reversed
for fusible appliqué.

Sugar Rush Small Flower Center

Sugar Rush
Large Flower Center
Enlarge 200%.
Trace 1.

Sugar Rush Large Flower Center

Sugar Rush
Small Flower
Enlarge 200%.
Trace 1.

Pattern is reversed
for fusible appliqué.

Sugar Rush Small Flower

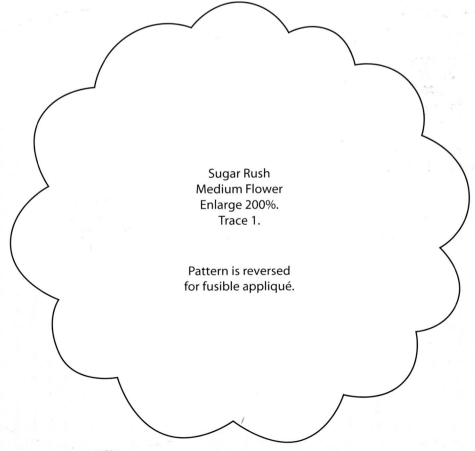

Sugar Rush
Medium Flower
Enlarge 200%.
Trace 1.

Pattern is reversed
for fusible appliqué.

Sugar Rush Medium Flower

a b c d e f
g h I j k l
m n o p q
r s t u v w
x y z

Happy-Go-Lucky Monogram Letters

Simply Blissful Fabrics

BY DESIGNER CAMILLE ROSKELLEY
FOR MODA FABRICS

FOLLOW MODA FABRICS ON TWITTER & FACEBOOK FOR THE NEWEST DESIGNS & PROJECTS.

moda
www.modafabrics.com

For a list of other fine books from C&T Publishing,
ask for a free catalog:

C&T Publishing, Inc.
P.O. Box 1456
Lafayette, CA 94549
800-284-1114

Email: ctinfo@ctpub.com
Website: www.ctpub.com

Tips and Techniques can be found at www.ctpub.com >
Consumer Resources > Quiltmaking Basics:
Tips & Techniques for Quiltmaking & More

C&T Publishing's professional photography
services are now available to the public.
Visit us at www.ctmediaservices.com.

For quilting supplies:

Cotton Patch
1025 Brown Avenue
Lafayette, CA 94549

Store: 925-284-1177
Mail order: 925-283-7883

Email: CottonPa@aol.com
Website: www.quiltusa.com

*Note: Fabrics used in the quilts shown may not be
currently available, as fabric manufacturers keep
most fabrics in print for only a short time.*

Simplify, simplify.
—Henry David Thoreau